DATE DUE

#47-0108 Peel Off Pressure Sensitive

Today's Superst★rs
Entertainment

Dwayne "The Rock" Johnson

by Jacqueline Laks Gorman

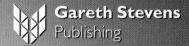

Gareth Stevens
Publishing

Please visit our web site at: www.garethstevens.com
For a free color catalog describing Gareth Stevens Publishing's
list of high-quality books, call 1-800-542-2595 (USA)
or 1-800-387-3178 (Canada).

Library of Congress Cataloging-in-Publication Data

Gorman, Jacqueline Laks.
    Dwayne "the Rock" Johnson / Jacqueline Laks Gorman.
        p. cm. — (Today's superstars: entertainment)
    Includes bibliographical references and index.
    ISBN: 978-0-8368-8200-1 (lib. bdg.)
    1. Rock (Wrestler). 2. Wrestlers—United States—Biography.
 3. Motion picture actors and actresses—United States—Biography. I. Title.
GV1196.R63G67   2008
796.812092—dc22   2007005190

This edition first published in 2008 by
Gareth Stevens Publishing
A Weekly Reader® Company
1 Reader's Digest Road
Pleasantville, NY 10570-7000 USA

Copyright © 2008 by Gareth Stevens, Inc.

Editor: Gini Holland
Art direction and design: Tammy West
Picture research: Diane Laska-Swanke

Photo credits: Cover, © Steve Azzara/CORBIS SYGMA; pp. 5, 7 © Duomo/
CORBIS; p. 8 © 20th Century Fox Film Corp./courtesy Everett Collection;
pp. 10, 11 © Peter Lederberg and Brian Berkowitz; pp. 12-13 © Collegiate
Images/Getty Images; p. 15 © Seth Browarnik/WireImage.com; p. 17 © Collegiate
Images, LLC/WireImage.com; p. 18 © AP Images; p. 21 The Everett Collection;
p. 22 © Kevin Mazur/WireImage.com; p. 24 © Universal/courtesy Everett
Collection; p. 26 © John Parra/WireImage.com; p. 27 © Djamilla Rosa
Cochran/WireImage.com; p. 28 © Regis Martin/Getty Images

Printed in the United States of America

1 2 3 4 5 6 7 8 9 11 10 09 08 07

Contents

Chapter 1

The Most Electrifying Man

More than nineteen thousand fans were crowded into the Kiel Center in St. Louis, Missouri. The date was November 15, 1998. Many more were seated in front of their television sets. They had paid to see the pay-per-view show. All of them were waiting for the *Survivor Series '98*, one of the top events in professional wrestling. The winner would become the champion of the World Wrestling Federation (WWF). Fourteen men would fight for the title. One of them was The Rock.

The Rock — whose real name is Dwayne Johnson — was only twenty-six years old. He had been in the WWF for only two years. Still, he was already one of the most popular wrestlers in the world.

He liked to call himself "the most electrifying man in sports entertainment."

Winning the Title

To win the title, Dwayne "The Rock" Johnson had to beat four other wrestlers in four matches. "Winning the *Survivor Series* requires strength, stamina, speed, and showmanship," he later said. The Rock showed all of them that night. First, he got past a wrestler called Big Boss Man. Then

he beat Ken Shamrock, and then The
Undertaker. Finally, he faced Mankind in
the title match. Their seventeen-minute
battle was a classic. The fight was full of
all the things that make professional
wrestling so exciting — sudden moves,
headlocks, flying elbows, and even chairs
being tossed around the ring. The Rock
was too much for Mankind, who quit.
The Rock was declared the new WWF
champion. Of course, because this
was professional wrestling, it had been
decided ahead of time that The Rock
would win. All of the other wrestlers
knew it and played along. Wrestling fans
also knew it, but they went along, too.

Nothing in pro wrestling, including
the *Survivor Series*, is "real." It's just a
show. A wrestler "wins" when he pins
the other guy at the end or makes him
give up. Nothing is judged or rated.

The Rock had won his first
championship title. By the time he
was done wrestling, he would
win the title seven times. He
has more titles than any

Fact File

The Rock thought a lot about
his "look" as a wrestler. Unlike
some wrestlers, he never wanted
to wear face paint, a mask, armor,
leather, or a cape.

The World of Professional Wrestling

Professional wrestling is part sports and part entertainment. The wrestlers are playing roles in a show. The storyline is decided ahead of time. The wrestlers know who will win and who will lose. They plan out all the moves together. As part of the show, different wrestlers join in groups to fight other groups of wrestlers. They also have long-standing fights, called feuds. The feuds are not real. For example, The Rock is very close friends with Stone Cold Steve Austin, who was his bitter enemy in the ring. Feuds, and all of the other things that go into pro wrestling, are carefully planned to entertain the fans.

Many wrestlers have special names and interesting personalities. The fans get to know them well as they follow their adventures in the ring. The wrestlers also tape promos for TV, which are announcements made to advertise events. The Rock was one of the most talented wrestlers when it came to doing promos. His promos were often as entertaining as his fights.

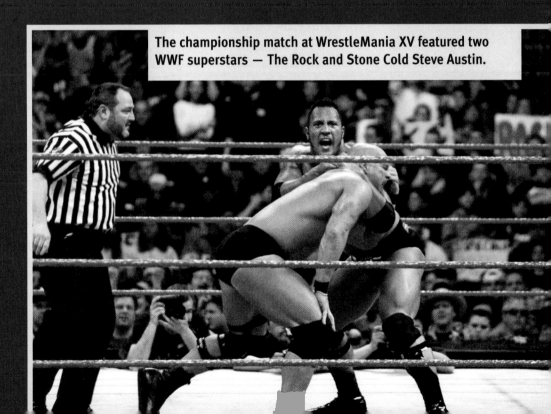

The championship match at WrestleMania XV featured two WWF superstars — The Rock and Stone Cold Steve Austin.

other man in the history of professional wrestling.

The Rock, however, was too big for the ring. His sense of humor, good looks, and stage presence led to offers to act in movies. The Rock had already conquered one arena. Now he was ready to become the next great action hero.

Fact File

The Rock is the first third-generation wrestler in the WWF. His father and grandfather were both well-known champion wrestlers.

Life on the Road

Dwayne Douglas Johnson was born on May 2, 1972, in Hayward, California. He was the only child of Rocky and Ata Johnson. Wrestling was part of his life from the beginning. Dwayne's father and his grandfather, Peter Maivia, were both professional wrestlers.

The Johnson family is made up of different races. Rocky, who was born in Canada, is black. Ata is from Samoa, which is an island in the Pacific Ocean. Dwayne was taught by his parents to respect and celebrate both parts of his background.

Traveling Days

Dwayne spent his early years living in many places. His family lived for a while wherever

9

Fact File

Rocky was wrestling. Then they moved on.

Dwayne enjoyed his life on the road. He went to all of his father's fights and knew all of the other wrestlers. He practiced wrestling moves and played with his father's championship belts. He dreamed of being a champion like his father and grandfather. "I was raised in this environment," he later said. "It was all I knew, all I can remember. There was never a time when wrestling wasn't part of my life. And so . . . I was a road warrior from the very beginning. . . . By the time I started

Changes in Professional Wrestling

Professional wrestling has changed a lot since the 1970s. Today, wrestling is a big business. It is run in the United States by a company called World Wrestling Entertainment, or WWE. (It used to be called the World Wrestling Federation, or WWF.) The top WWE wrestlers are superstars. They perform in front of large crowds. Millions of people watch them on television. Years ago, wrestling was a local business. Different people ran the sport in separate parts of the country. The wrestlers worked for them, mostly in small arenas in front of small crowds. The wrestlers lived and worked in specific places until fans got tired of them and stopped coming to see them. Then the wrestlers moved on to other places. Wrestling was shown on television, but on local stations. Few people watched the shows. In the early 1980s, a man named Vince McMahon Jr. changed all this. McMahon began to combine some of the local wrestling groups. He also paid a lot of money to wrestlers from other groups that he did not control. They joined his company, the WWF. McMahon also made wrestling more interesting for the fans. He developed personalities and background stories for the different wrestlers. He also got big national TV contracts. McMahon made pro wrestling into the entertainment sensation it is today.

The Rock's father, Rocky Johnson (*below, grinning*), was a professional wrestler from the late 1960s to the early 1980s. He won a number of titles and was known as "the Soulman."

kindergarten, I had already lived in five states."

Life wasn't all fun and games, however. Rocky and Ata made sure Dwayne went to school. They made sure he did his homework. Dwayne was often naughty and got into fights. His parents worked hard to teach him to control his temper. They taught him good values, such as knowing right and wrong. They also taught him to stand up for the things he believed in.

Football Star

The Johnson family moved to Bethlehem, Pennsylvania, when Dwayne was in high school. He went to Freedom High School and joined the track and football teams. The football team played against some tough teams. Years later, Dwayne said that by playing

Fact File

Dwayne lived in fifteen different states while he was growing up, including Hawaii, Florida, California, and Georgia. He even lived overseas in New Zealand.

against such good players he learned a lot about working hard and wanting to win.

Dwayne became one of the best defensive tackles in Pennsylvania. When he was a senior, many colleges sent people to talk to him. Each of them wanted Dwayne to go to their college so he could play on their football team. He was offered scholarships by many of the top schools in the country. Dwayne decided to go to the University of Miami in Florida.

Fact File

The wrestling coach at Freedom High School asked Dwayne to join the wrestling team. Amateur wrestling is very different from professional wrestling. Dwayne thought it was boring and too easy. He quit after just one day of practice.

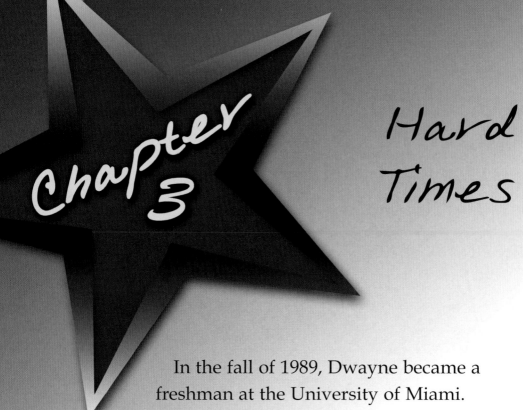

Chapter 3

Hard Times

In the fall of 1989, Dwayne became a freshman at the University of Miami. Many freshmen don't get to be starting players on top college teams. The coaches told Dwayne, however, that he was going to start for the Miami Hurricanes.

A Tough Break

A tough thing happened ten days before the first game of the season. Dwayne was badly hurt during practice. He needed to have an operation on his shoulder. He could not play that season. Dwayne was unhappy and angry. He also missed his parents. He should have worked hard to get better and he should have done his schoolwork. Instead, he drank, slept late, and did not go to his college classes.

In December, Dwayne's coach called him into the office. The coach told Dwayne that he had gotten a grade point average (GPA) of only 0.7. He had not even earned 1.0 grade point! The best GPA you can get is 4.0, so Dwayne had done very, very badly. He had failed most of his classes. "In that moment," he later said, "I felt about as worthless as I had ever felt in my life. I had let my parents down, I had let my teammates and coaches down, and I had let myself down." He was put on academic probation. He had to study hard to get his grades up. If he didn't, he would have to leave the team.

Soon, Dwayne had another reason to do better in school. He met a girl named Dany Garcia. Dany was four years older than Dwayne. She was smart and was studying finance. As soon as he met Dany, Dwayne

Dwayne and Dany Johnson share a happy moment in 2006. Dwayne has always thanked Dany for inspiring him to do well — both in college and in life.

knew that she was the girl for him.
He wanted her to be proud of him.

Football Triumph and Trouble

Dwayne went to all his classes, worked hard, and brought his grades up, so he was able to play the next year. He was part of the team when the Hurricanes won the 1991 national championship. They did it by beating Nebraska, 22–0, in the Orange Bowl on January 1, 1992. Dwayne continued to play well after that. He expected to be drafted by the National Football League when he graduated.

During his senior year, however, he hurt his back. He should have rested, but he kept playing. He did not play well because he was in so much pain. Dwayne was not drafted by the NFL. Instead, he got an offer from the Calgary Stampeders of the Canadian Football League. After he graduated in 1995, he went off to Canada. He hoped that he would play well there. Then maybe he could join the NFL in the future.

Fact File

Dany's parents were immigrants. They came from Cuba. They were not happy when she began to date someone who was half-black. They did not want to meet Dwayne for many years, until a few months before he and Dany got married.

The University of Miami Hurricanes

The University of Miami Hurricanes were one of the best
football teams in the United States in the late 1980s and
early 1990s. Dennis Erickson was the coach from 1989
to 1994. During those years, they won sixty-three games
and lost only nine. The Hurricanes won the national
championship in 1989 when they beat Alabama, 33–25.
They won the championship again in 1991 when they beat
Nebraska, 22–0. From 1985 to 1994, the Hurricanes set a
record for the longest home winning streak. They won
fifty-eight straight games. Dwayne had some great
teammates. For example, defensive tackle Warren Sapp is
one of the top players in the NFL today. He played with the
Tampa Bay Buccaneers and joined the Oakland Raiders in
2004. Linebacker Ray Lewis helped the Baltimore Ravens
win the Super Bowl in January 2001. Defensive tackle
Russell Maryland was the first pick in the NFL draft in 1991.
He played for ten years in the NFL with different teams.

During a 1993 game at the Orange Bowl Stadium in Miami, Dwayne (*on the right, center, number 94*) dashed to sack the Temple University Owls quarterback.

17

Dwayne had a terrible time in Canada. He was not on the regular team. He was on the practice squad, so he didn't get to play. He had very little money and shared a run-down apartment with some of his teammates. He slept on a used mattress he found in a dumpster. To get free food, he went to team meetings he did not have to attend — just so he could pick up a few sandwiches!

Then the Stampeders cut him from the practice squad. Dwayne had two choices.

He could try to make the team the next year, or he could give up his dream of playing football. He decided it was time to get into the family business. It was time to become a pro wrestler.

Baby-Faced Heel

Dwayne's parents had moved to Florida a few years before. He moved into their house now. He got a part-time job working in a health club, but he spent most of his time training to be a wrestler. From the beginning, Dwayne knew he had made the right decision. "It was crazy, but I knew in my heart that I had found my calling," he said.

Welcome to the WWF

Dwayne got a tryout with the WWF in early 1996. The people from the WWF liked what they saw. They gave Dwayne a contract to become a wrestler. They wanted him to get more training before he could fight for the WWF. To give him that training, they sent him to the United States Wrestling Alliance

(USWA) in Tennessee and then to their headquarters in Connecticut.

The WWF also wanted Dwayne to have a good wrestling name. They convinced him to call himself Rocky Maivia. That way, fans would remember his father and his grandfather.

On November 16, 1996, Dwayne made his official WWF debut at the *Survivor Series '96* in New York City. Eight wrestlers would fight until one of them won. The winner was the new guy — Rocky Maivia.

Dwayne was now a professional wrestler. He began to work regularly. He became friends with other wrestlers. He was successful from the start. On February 13, 1997, he won the Intercontinental Championship by beating Triple H. At the time, he was the youngest Intercontinental Champion in history.

Rocky Maivia was a typical baby face. He was very sweet and smiled a lot. The fans were supposed to like him, but a strange thing happened. The crowd turned against him and started to boo him. Rocky had trouble

Fact File

While Dwayne was wrestling with the USWA, he used the name Flex Kavana.

20

smiling when this happened. In August 1997, the WWF suggested that he "turn heel" and become a bad guy. He joined a group of bad-guy wrestlers called the Nation of Domination.

Enter The Rock

In December 1997, Rocky was going to face Stone Cold Steve Austin, who was one of the top wrestlers. Rocky challenged him during a promo. For the first time, he used the name "The Rock." He began to show a new personality. With that, a new wrestling superstar was born. The Rock was, in Dwayne's words, an "arrogant, self-centered,

Fact File

During Dwayne's tryout with the WWF, he wore purple trunks he borrowed from a retired wrestler. He also wore white boots he borrowed from his father.

The Ins and Outs of Wrestling

Pro wrestling matches are called works. During a match, the wrestlers are "selling." This means that they are trying to convince the fans that everything going on in the ring is real. A wrestler's opponent is really his partner, since they are acting out a story together. A referee is part of the show. He pretends to be in charge of the match. He also pretends to make sure the wrestlers don't use foreign objects, like tables or trash cans. Often, wrestlers do use these things. Often, the referee struggles with the wrestlers and winds up being part of the match.

Some wrestlers are heels, or bad guys. Others are baby faces, or good guys. Wrestlers often change these roles. Someone who is known as a baby face may suddenly become a heel. It is all done to give the fans a good show.

The Rock's last official WWF show was *WrestleMania XX* in 2004. He lost to Batista (*shown here lifting The Rock*) even though he fought like a winner.

but undeniably talented wrestler who couldn't care less what other people thought."

The Rock became amazingly popular. Fans loved his special lines, like "Do you smell what The Rock is cooking?" They loved the way he lifted his right eyebrow, which he called "the People's Eyebrow." The fans stayed with him when he left the Nation of Domination to join another group, called the Corporation. They stayed with him again when he was kicked out of the Corporation — as part of a WWF storyline — and became "the People's Champion."

New Experiences, New Opportunities

Dwayne had some new experiences away from the ring. He and Dany were married on May 3, 1997. Their wedding had both Cuban and Samoan traditions.

Dwayne had new opportunities, too. In 2000, he wrote a book called *The Rock Says . . .* , which became a best-seller. He had a small part in the movie *Longshot*. He was also

Fact File

Many of Dwayne's relatives were wrestlers. His uncles, Afa and Sika Anoai, were called the Wild Samoans. His cousins, Rodney Anoai (who was called Yokozuna) and Solofa Fatu Jr. (who was called Rikishi) were both champion wrestlers.

On the set of *The Scorpion King*, Dwayne and one of his co-stars, Grant Heslov (*center*) listen to Chuck Russell, the director (*left*). In the movie, Dwayne played a mighty warrior who is leading a group of rebels against an evil king.

Fact File

Dwayne received $5.5 million for making *The Scorpion King*. It set a record for the most money paid to an actor who is getting top billing for the first time.

in an episode of the TV series *Star Trek: Voyager*. A bigger acting role followed. Dwayne took time off from the WWF to appear as the Scorpion King in the movie *The Mummy Returns* (2001). In 2002, he played the same role in the movie *The Scorpion King*. This time, he was the star.

Leaving The Rock Behind

Chapter 5

The Rock did not wrestle as much when Dwayne's movie career took off. His last official appearance was in March 2004 at the pay-per-view *WrestleMania XX*. Dwayne's life was now taking a different course.

Exiting the Ring for the Screen

Dwayne appeared in several movies in 2004 and 2005. In *Walking Tall*, he played a soldier who returns to his hometown. He becomes the sheriff and tries to clean things up. In the crime comedy *Be Cool*, he played Vince Vaughn's bodyguard, who wants to be a singer. In *Doom*, he played a soldier who tries to stop an uprising on Mars.

Dwayne's biggest role was in the 2006 movie *Gridiron Gang*. He played Sean

Dwayne and his daughter, Simone, hosted a "Me and My Daddy" fashion show to raise money for a children's charity in 2006.

Porter, who runs a jail for troubled kids. Sean helps them by forming a football team. Dwayne said he could relate to the characters because he had been arrested when he was a teenager. Luckily, the police officer who arrested him got him to stay out of trouble by playing football.

Private and Public Lives

Dwayne and Dany live in Florida with their daughter, Simone Alexandra. She was born on August 14, 2001. Dany runs her own company, which helps people manage their money.

The Johnsons are active in social causes. Dwayne and Dany set up the Dwayne Johnson ROCK Foundation to help kids with different kinds of problems. One of its programs is called The Rock's Toy Chest. It puts toy boxes filled with special toys in playrooms at children's hospitals. In 2006, it gave $2 million to the University of Miami to build a living room in a new campus building. The room will be called the "Dany and Dwayne 'The Rock' Johnson Living

Fact File

Actor Michael Clarke Duncan, who was in the movie *The Scorpion King*, is one of Dwayne's best friends.

A Samoan High Chief

In 2004, Dwayne visited Samoa, his mother's homeland. He met the king, whose name is Malietoa Tanumafili II. The king crowned Dwayne as a high chief. He said that Dwayne would now have the title of Son of Malietoa, which means son of a king. "I told him I was going to carry this title with honor, dignity, and, above all else, with pride," Dwayne said.

Dwayne has a number of tattoos. The largest and most detailed is a Samoan tattoo on his left arm and chest. It tells the story of his life and family and the things that are important to him.

The Samoan tattoo on Dwayne's left arm and side shows the things and people he loves. He says the tattoo acts like a shield, protecting his family. Here, in 2004, he shows it proudly at *Wrestlemania XX* in Madison Square Garden.

Room." Dwayne is also involved in programs against drugs, racism, and AIDS.

Remembering the Fans

In 2006, Dwayne announced that he does not want to be called The Rock any more. "I am no longer a wrestler," he said. "I am now pursuing a future as an actor and some day as a director. I am not The Rock, I am Dwayne Johnson."

Still, it's hard to leave The Rock behind. For one thing, Dwayne can't forget his fans or the wrestling world. "I have so much love and respect for the fans," he said. "I'll never forget where I came from. I love the business. I grew up in the business. . . . Everyone always asks me what I miss about wrestling. Hands down, I miss the interaction with the fans. . . . Every night was a different crowd and they gave me so much energy, and I'll always love that and always miss that for sure."

Time Line

1972	Dwayne Douglas Johnson is born on May 2 in Hayward, California.
1995	Graduates from the University of Miami and joins the Calgary Stampeders of the Canadian Football League.
1996	Makes official WWF debut at *Survivor Series '96*.
1997	Takes the name The Rock; marries Dany Garcia.
1998	Wins first of seven WWF/WWE world championships.
2000	Writes the best-selling book *The Rock Says . . . .*
2001	Plays the role of Scorpion King in the movie *The Mummy Returns*.
2002	Receives top billing in the movie *The Scorpion King*.
2004	Makes last official wrestling appearance at *WrestleMania XX*.
2006	Stars in the movie *Gridiron Gang*; announces that he no longer wants to be called The Rock.

Glossary

academic probation — a period of time when a student must improve his or her grades.

defensive tackle — someone who plays a defensive position in football and tries to stop the other team from scoring.

finance — involved with managing money.

grade point average (GPA) — an average of a student's grades. An A has a value of 4, a B is 3, a C is 2, a D is 1, and an F is 0.

headlock — a wrestling position in which one wrestler holds another wrestler's head with his arm.

linebacker — a defensive football player whose position is behind the defensive line.

pay-per-view — paying a fee to watch a special television program on cable or satellite TV.

professional — one who receives money to do a job.

promo — an advertisement made to promote something or someone.

Samoa — an island state in the Pacific Ocean that is an independent country.

scholarship — money given to a student so he or she can attend school.

stamina — energy and strength that lasts for a long time during physical activity.

tattoo — a permanent design made on the skin by pricking it with needles and staining it with dye.

tryout — a test given to someone to see if he or she should be given a job, role, or position.

To Find Out More

Books

The Buzz on Professional Wrestling. Scott Keith
(Lebhar-Friedman Books)

Pro Wrestling: From Carnivals to Cable TV. Sports Legacy
(series). Keith Elliot Greenberg (LernerSports)

The Story of the Wrestler They Call "The Rock." Pro
Wrestling Legends (series). Dan Ross (Chelsea House)

Videos

Gridiron Gang (Columbia) PG-13

The Scorpion King (Universal) PG-13

Walking Tall (MGM) PG-13

Web Sites

Dwayne Johnson Fever
www.dwaynejohnsonfever.net/PhotoGallery/index.php
Photos of Dwayne Johnson

Hollywood Celebrity
www.hollywood.com/celebrity/Dwayne_Johnson/1117368
News, biography, photos, and an interview with
Dwayne Johnson

Index

About the Author

Jacqueline Laks Gorman has been a writer and editor for more than twenty-five years. She grew up in New York City and attended Barnard College and Columbia University, where she received a master's degree in American history. She has worked on many kinds of books and has written several series for children and young adults. She now lives in DeKalb, Illinois, with her husband, David, and children, Colin and Caitlin. They are not particularly big wrestling fans, but if they had to pick a favorite wrestler, it would be The Rock.